DATE DUE

DEMCO 38-296

MY HIROSHIMA

A PERSONAL EPIC

by

Richard J. Schoeck

**Co-Winner of First Place
1996 Mellen Poetry Prize**

R

MY HIROSHIMA

A PERSONAL EPIC

by

Richard J. Schoeck

Mellen Poetry Press
Lewiston•Queenston•Lampeter

Library of Congress Cataloging-in-Publication Data

Schoeck, Richard J.
    My Hiroshima : a personal epic / by Richard J. Schoeck.
        p. cm.
    Includes bibliographical references.
    ISBN 0-7734-2846-1 (paper)
    1. Hiroshima-shi (Japan)--History--Bombardment, 1945--Poetry.
    2. World War, 1939-1945--Japan--Poetry. 3. Atomic bomb victims-
    -Poetry. I. Title.
    PS3569.C52338M9   1997
    811'.54--dc21
                                                            97-30529
                                                              CIP

The Edwin Mellen Press   The Edwin Mellen Press
         Box 450   Box 67
    Lewiston, New York   Queenston, Ontario
    USA 14092-0450   CANADA L0S 1L0

The Edwin Mellen Press, Ltd.
Lampeter, Dyfed, Wales
UNITED KINGDOM SA48 7DY

Printed in the United States of America

In memory of my brother,
Robert J. Schoeck, 1st Lt., U.S.A.F.,
a navigator-bombardier
lost in the South Pacific
March 20, 1944

— and lost comrades in
the Paratroops and
106th Signal Company

TABLE OF CONTENTS

It takes a thousand voices to tell
a single story.

(Source unknown)

History, despite its wrenching pain,
cannot be unlived, but if faced with
courage, need not to be lived again.

Maya Angelou in her poem for
Inauguration Day (20 January 1993)

How shall we praise the magnificence of
the dead?

Conrad Aiken, *Tetélestai*

PROLOGUE

You shall forget these things, toiling in the household,
You shall remember them, droning by the fire,
When age and forgetfulness sweeten memory
Only like a dream that has often been told
And often been changed in the telling. They will seem unreal.
Human kind cannot bear very much reality.
T. S. Eliot, *Murder in the Cathedral*

❖ ❖ ❖ ❖ ❖ ❖

How can the awfulness of annihilation
be told? ... the agony of belief itself
destroyed when moments earlier people
were alive but now there is only death
and desolation? ...
We were all in uniform
elsewhere, all thought only of ourselves when
told of Hiroshima: *that ends the war,*
we said. Now we won't have to sail for Asia
and more years of serving in uniform.
Some may have thought like the poet in the first
World War,
Have we lost our way,
Or are we toys of a god at play,
Who do these things on a young spring day?
How could we in our early twenties know
that Borges would be wrong denying one
single time in which all events are linked?
The old world flowed into that huge meltdown
of nuclear science and technology
on August the 6th, 1945,
at Hiroshima. All human history
coaled together in that exploding atom

2

and its visible high mushrooming cloud.
Given what we were, with oaths to obey,
and what little we were told — we could not know
the flight of the alone to the Alone:
that man had reversed God's act of creation.
Nor could we question what we had been told
nor orders to celebrate properly.
— Was it the age-old *timor mortis*
conturbat me that numbed our consciences
collectively and in each one of us?
Or was it lack of patience to face up
to responsibilities of the war —
that, and being sick at heart with boredom
to the point of melancholy? (War
can be defined as long stretches of intense
boredom punctuated by brief moments
of intense fear.)
                                        I muse
today with another poet,
                        Was it so hard, Achilles,
                                So very hard to die?
The ringing answer clothed in discipline
('willing, immediate obeying orders')
enabled companies and platoons
to storm impossibilities, and then
in letting go of tension to endure.
Now I am seventy-five years of age
and winding down my life's clockwork,
but still consumed to seek and write the truth
and chart slow painful growth in consciousness:
in honesty before my children and my God
(searching memory's neglected attic) I
confront the questions of the dropping of the bomb.

CANTO I

WHAT IT WAS LIKE

Neither the world nor the scientists
are any longer innocent.
Source unknown

Bliss was it in that dawn to be alive,
And to be young was very heaven.
Wordsworth, The Prelude

Experience is never limited and it is never
complete; it is an immense sensibility,
a kind of huge spider's web of the silken
threads suspended in the chambers of consciousness
and catching every airborne particle
in its tissue. It is the very atmosphere
of the mind.
Henry James

Arma virumque cano...
Virgil, *Aeneid*, I.i.

To sing of arms and of the men who were
fugitives by fate — so were we all
whether inducted by the Selective Service
to serve at the will of the President,
or volunteers like me for private reasons
(the Regular Army a career choice,
and proud to be identified a dog-face) —
in either case we marched each one of us
to private appointments in Samarra,
so were we whistled down the corridors
of power by bureaucrats who signed
documents and by generals who gave
necessary commands for unfolding
situations, then made fresh strategies.

In putting on the uniform we lost
a portion of identity, surrendered
some measure of responsibility
to higher echelons of legitimate
authority. We could not question why —
civilians then or historians later
considering war retrospectively
(at a safe remove from time and place)
have rarely understood the simple
categorical imperative of command,
nor that a man in uniform is not
much encouraged to taste the luxury
of solipsism, that disease that eats
our contemporary American
society, nor may poets telling of war
enjoy the privilege of the grand style:

we know too much, as Churchill did, *the grim
and awful cataclysm of war.*

❖ ❖ ❖ ❖ ❖ ❖

In 1940 the Regular Army
numbered a scant two hundred thousand men
(including the Army Air Corps). We trained ...
the services all grew in size and moved
(but we saw only the leaves under the trees,
and lived in the dirt and mud underneath,
not seeing much of tree and less of forest)
towards readiness — we trained recruits, we built
a military in camps from Georgia
to California (Benning, Houston, Bragg, Sill,
Hood, Riley, Ord: old soldiers' pride rings out
in these and other names. But there were still
too many militasters and the process took time,
while the German armies rolled across vast space,
and Japanese succeeded everywhere in Asia).
I thank the Providence that gave us then
in the U.S. Army's Chief of Staff
General George C. Marshall's unique
coalescence of experience,
intelligence — and still more — integrity.
Slowly commanders were trained to command
on Carolina, Louisiana,
Tennessee and Texas maneuvers, plus
California desert and Colorado
mountains. In winter and summer we trained,
and we trained with one end in view: victory.
Democracies must know that there are times
to *militate*: the word carries its freight

of meaning (from *miles*) to serve as soldier —
a Latin word, with Roman sense of duty.

❖ ❖ ❖ ❖ ❖ ❖

Night March in Training

Time past and time ahead
are the beginning and the end
of time present, and history
is written of the present time
in the future when it will be past.

But these are only words,
this thought the outward echo
of my inner world of speculation.
Shall I ever understand the war
more perfectly than now, or see
more clearly the slow meaning
heart breaking? On the horizon,
over the hill, through the woods,
our long column marches —
friends I knew but hollow men
whose bodies like mine
are exhausted beyond despair.
(I fell asleep in ranks
marching, going up hill,
and wakened with a stumble when
we began the long descent
and the pain of broken bones
in both my feet increased.)
Could I ever want memory
to live incredibly again
this endless night march?

But these things I have spoken
I have told for you to remember
when the time for remembrance comes.

❖ ❖ ❖ ❖ ❖ ❖

Even in training there were casualties,
and from a training jump I went to hospital,
and later there were nightmares peopled with faces
matching airborne casualties in Normandy:

> *No manifesto, one command,*
> *and we were out, our squad,*
> *straight from the door we jumped —*
> *I checked (Thank God!) the chute*
> *yawning overhead, close and tight*
> *(as stomach's fear of fear)*
> *carved against the black of night*
> *wonder of its being there, the silk ...*
> *I rode upon the wind the clear*
> *incredible delight of space,*
> *knew air the element of heart*
> *intense and great with laughing face,*
> *lost touch with now and here.*
>
> *Out of the sleepless night*
> *I swing in harness on the air,*
> *nearer, in darkness of the mind,*
> *to comrades died ...*
>   *cite*
> *the day, the battle, the campaign,*
> *still the mornings, the nights remain,*
> *with the laughter, the strength,*
> *the swinging chutes upon the wind.*

9

❖ ❖ ❖ ❖ ❖ ❖

And slowly I had news of casualties
inflicted on the brave 106th in Belgium
in the Battle of the Bulge, and from hospital
at Atterbury I heard reports of men
who died those first shattering three days —
                                      more
in POW camps as I learned later.

And by 1945 with Europe won
our minds were now turned towards Japan.
The optimists thought that we might defeat
the enemy in two years, or three;
the pessimists thought it would take five
or longer to finish off the invasion,
that casualties would be incalculable,
innumerable as the summer mosquitoes
plaguing us in training and on maneuvers.
But at that time I had no access to
the estimates of generals at the Pentagon.
Yet some of us at Army schools had heard
rumors that ranged from two hundred thousand
to a million casualties — rumor (as Virgil
said) thrives on movement gathering strength
and marches on the ground until it hides
its head among the clouds. "You do two things
with a rumor," went the GI phrase, "you don't
believe it yourself, and you pass it on."

I had been made aware of Holmes' words
(thrice-wounded Union officer, he spoke
Memorial Day in 1884):

The generation that carried on the war
has been set apart by its experience.
Through our great good fortune, in our youth
our hearts were touched with fire. It was given
to us to learn at the outset that life
is a profound and passionate thing.... We
have seen with our own eyes, beyond and above
the golden fields, the snowy heights of honor,
and it is for us to bear the report
to those who come after us.
                                    So may it be.
The Air Corps trained to produce fliers,
pilots, navigators, bombardiers and crews
across those crowded years ... My brother
trained in Carolina, Alabama, New Mexico,
and California; then went to the South Pacific,
from which he did not return. Across the camps
and fields of Carolina, Georgia, Alabama,
California, I've heard their voices lifted high
to sing their song:
                    Off we go into the wild blue yonder
                    ... with one helluva roar ...
                    The Army Air Corps ...

❖ ❖ ❖ ❖ ❖ ❖

The Plane

The Superfortress was forged in four years,
first flown in '42 and built at five plants
around the U.S. Within only two years
it was operational in the Pacific
often in flights of up to 500 planes;
by war's end over four hundred 29s

11

were lost in combat and operational
accidents, with more than 3,000 crewmen
killed, wounded or missing — a plane
conceived for hazards of Pacific war.
When production ceased in '46, nearly
four thousand of the proud 29s had been built.

Now the plane to fly the atom bomb
from Pacific bases was ready. Next
the airbase was put in place: July '44
Saipan fell to the Americans, thus
Tokyo was now in range of bombers,
beginning in November '44.
A smaller island, Tinian, across
the Saipan channel (100 miles north
of Guam, six thousand from San Francisco)
was chosen to be the largest airport in
the world: six ten-lane runways each almost
two miles long were built by the military
in less than one year. The operation
waited only for the final training, and the bomb.

❖ ❖ ❖ ❖ ❖ ❖

The Men to Fly the Planes

The command pilot Lawrence Tibbets, then
only thirty years of age but a veteran
of North African and Europe bombing missions
and integral to the testing program of B-29s,
already was one of America's most experienced
fliers. A group was organized under him,
the legendary 509th Composite Group

12

of the 313th Wing of the 21st
Bomber Command. In January '45
Curtis LeMay (*a chewer of cigars* and tough:
you've got to kill people, that's what war's
about) — took over the Bomber Command
and changed the tactics radically, the planes
now flew at night, at very low altitudes,
and the aircraft were stripped of guns and ammunition
with three fewer crewmen — only the tail gunner
was kept to protect against attacks from the rear —
and the bomb-load was raised from three to six tons
(mostly incendiaries for the bombing
of the combustible cities of Japan).
Thus in March of '45 LeMay's bombers made
a fire-bombing campaign, and in the next five months
destroyed half of 66 cities, but
leaving Hiroshima, Kokura,
Niigata and Nagasaki for the atom bombs.
All that winter and spring of '45
Tibbets trained his crews in the bleak Utah
desert (rats, rancid drinking water, termites
and isolation there) working in strictest secrecy.
Around that Group (75 planes in fifteen
flight crews) was a large ground crew of nearly
two thousand, all skilled in servicing the '29.
In Utah bombardiers were trained to work
by sight, without the customary radar,
and were dependent on clear weather — the mission
to drop the atom bomb consequently, so
the strategists decided, would be daring
day strikes. The building of the bomb was all
that remained in this great complex plan.

❖ ❖ ❖ ❖ ❖ ❖

CANTO II

THE MAKING OF THE BOMB

The original spark [was] kindled by Prometheus
               W. L. Laurence, *Dawn Over Zero*

Taken as a story of human achievement,
and human blindness, the discoveries in
the sciences are among the great epics.
               J. Robert Oppenheimer

What has been done is the greatest
achievement of organized science in history.
               President Harry S Truman (6 August 1945)

For ancient Greeks it was Prometheus,
one of the twelve great elemental Titans
who stole fire from Zeus' hiding place: the god
of fire Greeks thought him, but he paid a price
when Zeus chained him everlastingly to rock
and each day sent an eagle to consume
his immortal liver — in more than mortal pain
the fire-giver's liver constantly
regenerated itself.
                                    Out of shadows
of centuries the playwright Aeschylus
(always absorbing, subsuming, remaking)
in *Prometheus Bound* made him not only
the bringer of fire and civilization
to mankind but also (his name in Greek
originally meant Forethinker) he was
the preserver of men in that he gave
to them all the arts and sciences, all
means for spirit's survival as well as body's:
heat to cook and make a thousand utensils
and artifacts, and light producing knowledge.

❖ ❖ ❖ ❖ ❖ ❖

Two millenia ago Lucretius next
followed his master Epicurus
in explaining physical change in terms
of changeless atoms endlessly added to,
subtracted, or re-arranged. Even the soul,
Lucretius thought, was made of exceedingly
fine atoms body-bred and at its death
like smoke upon the air dissipated.
But that was philosophy, not science,

not grounded in experiment. Yet Virgil
praised Lucretius' quest in that great line,
Happy is he who knows the causes of things.

❖ ❖ ❖ ❖ ❖ ❖

Older even than that long Latin poem
of Lucretius, *De rerum natura,*
the Greeks conceived of atoms and saw
these moving in a plurality of worlds
through infinite space. Divinity breathed
upon Lucretius' conceiving Love
to be the generating, binding force,
whom he invoked to share his enterprise,
embraced more ancient powers of Aphrodite
and had also powers of Venus Genetrix,
bringer of Victory, the ballooning myth
fed by Aeneas' prayers to her and by
his role in founding the city of Rome.
We are not obliged to take her trappings
in fable and art as essential to
her core meaning, but we must accept her energy
and try to understand Love as a cosmic source
of power in the heavens and the world
as conceived by classical Roman poets.

❖ ❖ ❖ ❖ ❖ ❖

One figure dominated science then
before the war, Einstein, whom I saw in post-war
Princeton from time to time walking sometimes
alone on an ordinary street his head
wreathed in a halo-helmet of white hair
(an aureole around a splendid lion's

head) in a loose sweatshirt or baggy coat —
I talked once with him, but I always was
aware of the astronomical gap
in knowledge separating me from him.
He had been born in Ulm, not far from where
my grandfather came and Hermann Hesse's Calw:
he was a Swabian and looked like one,
perhaps a watchmaker in a provincial town
(like well-named Freudenstadt in the Black Forest):
he gave a sense of strength, simplicity,
and openness. His fellow physicist
Szilard made note that when he spoke to him
of possibilities of chain reaction
Einstein burst forth *Daran habe ich gar nicht
gedacht* ('I never thought about that'), but
he was willing to take responsibility.
The old paradigm of sun revolving round
the earth had long since given way to new:
earth had been put in proper place in solar terms:
thus old paradigms give way to new ones.
Within the lifetime of one man, a prophet
of the new science, a new testament
and scientific revolution had occurred
profounder far than Galileo's or Darwin's.

❖ ❖ ❖ ❖ ❖ ❖

The classic physics that I was taught first
in high school then in university
during the mid-thirties was cold stuff scarcely
warmed by mediocre teachers, and it gave
little sense of the excitement boiling
behind Einstein's furrowing of brow, or
at the half-dozen scientific centers:

Cambridge, where Rutherford numbered eleven
future Nobel Laureates among his students
and where the Cavendish Lab was the world's
center for experimental physics,
doubtless because Rutherford had patience
to listen to any young man with ideas;
Göttingen, where Born had his institute
in buildings funded by Rockefeller,
five future Nobelists were there: Wigner,
Heisenberg, Pauli, Fermi, and Franck, where
Oppenheimer gained his doctorate and won
admittance to the republic of science
(as Michael Polyani conceived science
should be, essentially mutual, with
a network sending ideas at speed of light).
Essentially mobile, too: for Rutherford
had moved from Canada at turn of century
(it was McGill research that won for him
the Nobel prize in 1908)
to Manchester, and finally Cambridge.
Seven remarkable scientists came
from the Hungarian Jewish middle class:
von Kármán, de Hevesy, Polanyi, Szilard,
Teller, Wigner and von Neumann — de Hevesy
and Wigner to win Nobel Prizes. One
of this generation of giants led
research at Los Alamos, having
published a mortal man's lifework of research
from '26 to '29 in quantum theory
and experimental astrophysics:
J. Robert Oppenheimer, polymath
and lover of Sanskrit, Greek and modern poetry.

❖ ❖ ❖ ❖ ❖ ❖

In June of '42 the president
transferred the project for development
of the atomic bomb to Army's Corps
of Engineers, and it devised the name
of Manhattan Engineer District for cover,
and General Groves was named the head, with power
hitherto undreamed of in democracy.
Massive industrial facilities
would be required to separate the small
quantities of fishionable uranium
and plutonium that even one bomb
would need. The Project at its peak of work
in 1944 employed well over
one hundred thousand people — at Hanford,
Washington, for heavy water, along
the Columbia River screened behind
Gable Mountain; in Tennessee, the plant
to separate U 235 from
U238 in quantity (Oak Ridge, but called Dog Patch);
and laboratories at Columbia
and Chicago. And finally Los Alamos
for the bomb's design: a deep canyon
some thirty miles northwest of Santa Fe,
an odd community in isolation
and total military security.
There was barbed-wire safeguarding around
the place; but inside, scientific freedom —
and Oppenheimer ran the lab and had
responsibility for security.
Odd it was, but it became instant community,
and men like Bethe came, and Philip Morrison
(a young student of Oppenheimer's) and
others and their families, for schools were planned
and there was provision for libraries

20

and movies, and other facilities.
                    (Bethe was still at Cornell in '49
                    when I arrived, and I met Phil Morrison
                    there; but the Project was very much
                    a secret from the public and the bomb
                    was not talked about by humanists —
                    I never broached the subject then with either
                    scientist, having family worries and
                    concerns for getting on with my career
                    I gave too little time to humanity.)
During the war the Manhattan Project
kept at its work unknown to others (even
to a Signal Corps officer in Manhattan),
and it was called a separate state with its
peculiar sovereignty, meticulously
planned and coordinated towards the end
of making an atomic bomb that theoretically
could end the war. The cost was great (even,
for that age, astronomical): it was
two billion dollars, secretly committed
and accounted for, like everything about
the Project's planning and administration.

❖ ❖ ❖ ❖ ❖ ❖

 One man of hundreds who worked on the bomb,
Alexander Langsdorf (died this year
at 83) was among seventy scientists
who petitioned Truman not to use the bomb.
Three decades after war was ended he was
in Japan consulting at Tohoku
University; when his train stopped near
the Hiroshima shrine and other travellers
got off the train, this scientist (his wife

recalled) *just sat there with tears in his eyes.*
His contribution was a single speck
of precious plutonium produced from
a cyclotron (an atomic-particle
splitter built for medical research), and it
was used in tests at Los Alamos.

❖ ❖ ❖ ❖ ❖ ❖

There had to be one final experiment,
a testing of structures of theory.
A flat mesquite and yucca-haunted desert
stretched more than fifty miles to the northwest
of Almagordo between the Rio Grande
and the Sierra Oscura was the place;
the atom bomb test was called Trinity.
Towers, bunkers, cameras were put in place,
elaborate were the preparations
made. Explosion happened proving theory
was right, some on the desert thought it might
set fire to the whole atmosphere, thus
burn away and finish off the earth.
The 16th of July of 'forty-five ...
The atom bomb test was called Trinity.
That living necessarily leads to death
all men must know, but Donne constructed the truth
and sang that death doth touch the Resurrection;
and Oppenheimer also had in mind
Donne's Holy Sonnet on the Trinity:
Batter my heart, three-person'd God — with force
to breake, blowe, burn and make: a new world
to explore possibilities of redemption
after destructive forces be released.
When Trinity went off in the New Mexico

dawn Oppenheimer thought of Hindu scripture
and this passage from the *Bhagavad-Gita*
where Vishnu is trying to persuade the Prince
to do his duty and, taking on his multi-armed form,
he says,

> *If the radiance of a thousand suns*
> *Were to burst at once into the sky*
> *That would be like the splendor of the Mighty One...*
> *Now I am become Death,*
> *The shatterer of Worlds —*

and the world would never again be the same.
After the War, in making a speech Oppenheimer
said he thought of Alfred Nobel's vain hope that
his dynamite would put an end to wars;
then of the legend of Prometheus, giving man
new powers, and with those powers, guilt
and recognition of potential evil:
that infinitely sad and haunted look
that I was to see in Oppenheimer's eyes
was that of one who had gazed deep into
the heart of darkness of the human race.

❖ ❖ ❖ ❖ ❖ ❖

Fission had been achieved, the theory worked,
and now the atom bomb was ready for
the drop.
             It needed only political
decision of the new president and then
a military choice of target. "This is
the greatest thing in history," Truman
exulted, and he added his resolve
to recommend to Congress ways to make
atomic power a force towards world peace.

23

CANTO III

THE DECISION
TO DROP THE BOMB

O, it is excellent
To have a giant's strength, but it is tyrannous
To use it like a giant.

Shakespeare, *Measure for Measure*, II.ii.

Power tends to corrupt,
and absolute power corrupts absolutely.

Lord Acton

To be cut off from the history of a problem
is like diagnosing a patient without a case
history. Political scientists and philosophers
alike must respect history at least as much as
a clinical physician.

Source unknown

The Atomic Age announced in 1932
was truly born in 1945,
early on 16 July on semi-
desert west of Almogordo:
one observer thought it was the nearest thing
to doomsday anyone could imagine;
another felt *as though one were present
at the moment of creation when God said*
'Let there be light.'
                    The apparatus worked,
and now the bombing of Japan became
an operational problem.
                    And so their marvellous constructs
                    of mind became
                    the intricately fashioned things
                    that crossed the line
                    of only-theoretically
                    possible machines:

                    what they once undertook to do
                    in laboratories at Columbia,
                    Los Alamos and Berkeley
                    they brought to pass:
                    the atom had been smashed,
                    and fission harnessed,
                    an atomic bomb been made
                    and two of them were on the way.

                    One might murmur like Yeats,
                    *All things hang like a drop of dew
                    upon a blade of grass.*

                    ❖ ❖ ❖ ❖ ❖ ❖

The echelons of command were in place:
Marshall in Washington (who favored a
well-designed demonstration against a
military target and not the bombing
of civilians) and the Pacific galaxy
of generals under Spaatz, with Groves commanding
the Manhattan Project, charged with research
design and delivery of atomic bombs.

For Einstein, Oppenheimer and others
their line of authority led through Groves
up to the President — the Roosevelt
who gave atomic physicists assurances
but died three months before the Almogordo
test leaving a Truman ill-prepared, who
knew nothing of Manhattan or convenants
about the uses of the bomb to be created.
For Tibbetts and his crews the chain of command
moved through LeMay and Arnold up to Marshall
and the Secretary of War, Henry Stimson,
an honorable man (like Acheson at State):
"The chief lesson I have learned in a long life,"
he wrote after the war, "is that the only way
you can make a man trustworthy is to trust him;
and the surest way to make him untrustworthy
is to distrust him and to show your distrust."
Few politicians (or generals) learned or practiced
this ancient wisdom. ...
                    But lines of influence
lay well concealed from all our eyes outside
the corridors of power at the Pentagon
and White House. Regarded as assistant president,
James F. Byrnes (*a vigorous extrovert*, experienced,
ambitious) stood out among those surrounding

the newly-installed Truman as he faced
the making of the decision to use
the atomic bomb while he prepared to meet
Stalin and Churchill at Potsdam that summer
(July 15th selected as a late-as-possible date).

❖ ❖ ❖ ❖ ❖ ❖

LeMay had ordered firebombs on Tokyo
(Dresden had been firebombed on February 13th
with devastating effect, and Americans
experienced the frightful cost of Iwo Jima
one week later: a casualty ratio of 2 to 1,
the highest in Marine Corps history).
He sanctioned firebombs on Tokyo:
(ruthless and barbaric killing of civilians,
some called it), and conferences of generals
went on galore, yet MacArthur, who saw
no military justification for dropping the bomb,
had not been consulted. A roll-call of the higher ups
involved in arriving at the bomb-dropping decision
must include Secretary of War Stimson
(a Nestor of the old school, like Acheson later).
The argument was made (and it would be reviewed
ad infinitum that far fewer people were killed
than if we had to invade — Japanese as well as
Americans — and that the war was shortened).
Marshall was an honorable man, and ten years
after Hiroshima he set forth his judgment:
>   *We had to end the war. We had to save American lives.*
>   *We had to halt this terrific expenditure of money*
>   *which was reaching a stupendous total.*
>   *And there was no way to economize on it*

28

until we stopped the war. The bomb stopped the war.
Therefore it was justifiable.
An epic can be told of Tibbett's crew,
the Superfortress and he flew from Tinian
on August 6, 1945 — the ship
he named *Enola Gay* after his mother.
But the dropping of the bomb must be
more quickly told although for bravery
there were epic proportions.
The plane was manufactured in Omaha,
Nebraska, and then modified (keeping
only its tail guns to save weight);
its name *Enola Gay* was painted on only
the night before the mission by its pilot.

❖ ❖ ❖ ❖ ❖ ❖

After the briefing there was a prayer by
the chaplain, Captain William B. Downey,
of the Hope Lutheran Church, Minneapolis:
> *Almighty Father, who wilt hear the prayers*
> *of them who love Thee, we pray Thee to be*
> *with those who brave the heights of Thy*
> *heavens and who carry the battle to our enemies.*
> *Guard and protect them, we pray Thee,*
> *May they, as well as we, know Thy Strength*
> *and power, and armed with Thy might may they*
> *bring this war to a rapid end. We pray Thee*
> *that the end of war may come soon, and*
> *once more we may know peace on earth. May*
> *the men who fly this night be kept safe*
> *in Thy care, and may they be returned safely*
> *to us. We shall go forward trusting in Thee,*
> *knowing we are in Thy care now and for ever. Amen.*

29

There is here the echoing (and adapting
for the war) of the prayer of St. John Chrysostom:
> *Fulfil now, O Lord, the desires and petitions*
> *of Thy servants, as may be most expedient for them.*

❖ ❖ ❖ ❖ ❖ ❖

On the appointed August day the strategy
was set: three planes took off one hour early,
at 1:45, the next morning, to act
as weather reporters. A second flight
of three planes was designated, one
of which was the strike plane piloted by
Tibbets himself, to take off at 2:45
and assembled over Iwo Jima
about fifteen minutes after daybreak.

The *Enola Gay* was 15,000 pounds
over designated takeoff weight, and Tibbets
used the whole of the long runway to take off.
Final assembly of the bomb began on board,
and it was activated two hours before release.
At 7:15 AM (an hour earlier Hiroshima time)
the weather scout plane made his report to
Tibbets that cloud cover made a visual bombing
of the city possible. The target,
Tibbets then told his crew, was Hiroshima,
and the plane's control was surrendered to
the bombardier Ferebee and the navigator van Kirk.
The Norden bombsight took the pilot's data
on wind speed and altitude and automatically
made course corrections. At 8:14 Hiroshima time
control of both the plane and bomb were turned
to the bombsight, and one minute later it dropped the bomb.

Tibbets took back the plane's controls and made
the much-practiced violent escape turn.
A flash of light filled the cockpit eleven
miles from the blast, and the first of two shock waves
hit the plane. Tibbets announced to his crew:
"Fellows, you have just dropped the first atomic bomb."

After the explosion the blast was many-colored,
and the first cloud reached about 8,000 feet.
The cloud began to mushroom, then went up
almost at once to 20,000 feet
until the top part of the cloud broke off,
eventually reaching 30,000 feet.
Several hundred miles away from Hiroshima
the column of smoke could still be seen piercing
so sharply into the early morning sky.
As Tibbets tamped down tobacco in his pipe
he commented to his co-pilot, Bob Lewis,
"I think this is the end of the war."

❖ ❖ ❖ ❖ ❖ ❖

Two hundred officers and men awaited
the return of the *Enola Gay*, and it set down
twelve hours and thirteen minutes after
its departure from Tinian. There General Spaatz,
commander of Strategic Air Forces,
and *all the ranking military brass*
that could be mustered in the Marianas
at that time met the disembarking crew.
Spaatz greeted Tibbets, shook his hand, and pinned
a Distinguished Service Cross to Tibbets'
rumpled overalls.

A member of the 509th,
Sergeant Harry Barnard, wrote a poem about
Atomic Might with this concluding stanza:

> *Oh, God — that when this War doth cease*
> *And again we turn our thoughts to peace*
> *That you will help us build — not devastate,*
> *A life of love and truth, — not hate,*
> *Without the thunderous blast, the blinding light*
> *Of the 509th's atomic might.*

❖ ❖ ❖ ❖ ❖ ❖

One entire nation was then involved
in the making and the dropping of the bomb,
although there could be no democracy
in time of war when even Truman (although
vice-president) knew nothing of the two-
billion dollar project called Manhattan,
and generals and their epigones pursued
their military strategies and private agendas.

❖ ❖ ❖ ❖ ❖ ❖

Scholastic philosophers, we are told,
debated seriously how many angels
could dance upon the head of a pin.
We smile, of course, at such ridiculousness:
does it matter? and how could you tell?
or, what do we learn from such an exercise
(if it really did take place in Paris,
Salamanca, Oxford or Cologne)?

But consider, if you will, in this good year
implications of such questions for our case.

If Operation Desert Storm was just —
forgive us, good King Henry the Fifth,
for retracing ground you've covered well before —
then does it not follow that each Christian
is obliged to follow orders of his sovereign?
And if just war is joined, will not there be
divine assistance? And if so, what better way
than by having dancing on the electronic nose
of each laser-guided bomb, an angel — or
a hierarchy of them — to lend assistance
in this alien world of computerization?
The question, you must agree, is not quite idle
and it could lead us to ask if any angel
followed the drop downwards from the *Enola Gay*
to achieve the desolation of the atomic blast.

CANTO IV

AT HIROSHIMA

The poetry is in the pity.
                    Wilfred Owen

... Hiroshima made light of human bones ...
                    Seamus Heaney, *Spirit Level* (1996)

The world never learns. History has a way
                    of making the past palatable, the dead
a dream ...
                    Richard Hugo, "Letter to Simic from Boulder"

That Monday morning, August 6th, had dawned
brightly, sunny and hot, and people were
on their way to work when the alarm sounded.
A single B-29 appeared in the sky,
and some small boys cried out, "B-29!"
It was the weather plane of Captain Eatherly,
and nothing happened. Then one hour later
the *Enola Gay* approached, accompanied
by two other B-29s, and at
8:15 its bomb was dropped and detonated
five hundred eighty meters over Shima
Hospital. No one, no living thing had ever
experienced the shock of such explosive power.
First came the lightning-bright flash, like splitting
of the sun. Next came the intolerable heat
that was ten thousand degrees centigrade
near the bomb's epicenter. Next came the noise
described as rumblings of volcanos or thousands
of artillery pieces, reverberating
beyond the city over hilltops shaking
towns surrounding. Next came the wind
with blows that knocked inhabitants to ground
and tore off their clothes. Then there was the fire
springing everywhere destroying consuming
eating bodies to the bone (the fire-god
was hungry, and his fire lasted two days).

Enveloping the light and heat and noise
and wind and fire was a huge unseen force
that sucked up everything into a cloud
of darkness breeding death that mounted to
that evergrowing frantic yet majestic
mushrooming. Afterwards there was the rain
(the huge drops filled with cinders, soot and dust)

but this was no salvation miracle
blessed by protecting gods. Instead each drop
came down from the cresting thirty thousand feet
of that atomic mushroom, bringing down to earth
those radio-active elements that
generated radiation disease.

❖ ❖ ❖ ❖ ❖ ❖

The horror must be known in human terms:
the blinding, maiming, burning, vaporising . . .
sixty-six thousand men, women, children
killed immediately or died soon afterwards.
That many more, so horribly injured:
suffering radiation sickness — many
lingered in their dying. Others carried
mutations in their genes, affecting unborn
generations. The suffering untold,
immeasurable by any calculus
of pain, incalculable their psychological
suffering: the *hibakusha*,
explosion-affected persons they are called.
At the epicenter of the city's heart
four square miles were utterly destroyed.

❖ ❖ ❖ ❖ ❖ ❖

The principal of Hiroshima's girl's
high school tells:
>   *I was burned and bandaged, and I went*
>   *to the work site. Many of the students'*
>   *eyeballs were popped out, their mouths ripped open*
>   *by the blast, their faces burned, hair gone,*
>   *clothes burned off; the girls' school uniforms*

37

were burned off completely; they were completely
stripped ... naked. It was just like, well,
a scene from hell.
But life had gone beyond Doré's illustrations
that vividly illustrate Dante's *Inferno*.
A watch worn by a casualty whose body burned
to a crisp remains set at 8:15 AM.
There are other records, to be sure, but
one cannot forget that human evidence —
nor the shadow made by some person sitting
on the steps in front of the Hiroshima Branch
of the Sumitoma Bank: he doubtless
died on the spot, in a single flashing moment,
the surface of the stone around where he sat
was whitened by exposure to the heat rays
of the bomb, where he sat rested dark,
a shadow of a person who once lived.
The bomb dropped on Hiroshima was three meters long
and less than one meter in diameter,
and it weighed four metric tons. Not huge, perhaps,
but it contained ten to thirty kilograms
of Uranium 235, of which
only one kilogram actually fissioned.
The A-bomb detonated about 1500 feet
above the ground, creating a monstrously huge
fireball, at the epicenter of which the temperature
reached several million degrees centigrade —
hotter than the sun by far. Then
there was the mushrooming cloud that everyone
has seen in films and photos of the bombing.
The heat was more than human beings could bear
to watch: iron melts at 1500 degrees centigrade,
and this one was two or three times hotter still.
Within a kilometer granite was bleached white,

and the quartz in the stone popped and made the
surface rough. Clothing, whether worn or drying
in the sun, spontaneously burst into flames,
within two kilometers of the hypocenter.
And railroad ties and wooden fences along railroads
up to two kilometers from the hypocenter
instantly ignited, and they burned. Trees
spontaneously combusted in the parks, and many
of the older trees burned from the inside out
and were left standing with only exterior trunks remaining.

A student in a middle school was in a classroom
during the bombing and managed to escape
the collapsed school building.
> "*A friend yelled B-29,*"
I remember, "*and that instant a flash pierced my eyes.*
At once the whole building collapsed and we
were trapped underneath. My face and hands throbbed
with pain. My front teeth were broken and my shirt
was soaked in blood. The school was nowhere to be seen:
it had vanished and only smoking ruins remained. Beyond
the school I could see only a sea of flames.
I was so terrified that I couldn't stop shaking,
But I finally worked free of the collapsed school,
and making sure to head upwind to escape the fires,
I made my way through the rubble of the city,
staggering haphazardly somehow escaped."
The fires in the city reached a peak mid-afternoon,
and they continued to burn until the end of the day,
covering the entire city. In all directions from
the center, ruins were melted together like lava
and distorted from the intense heat. In all directions
there was a scorched plain, desolate, inhuman.
They remembered the firestorms and whirlwinds,

and then the black rain — the ashes of death — that fell
like rain in the form of radioactive soot and dust,
and contaminated everything and everyone even in remote areas.

❖ ❖ ❖ ❖ ❖ ❖

How many? It is not known exactly how many people
were in the city that day, because of movements
of the military and evacuations, but it is believed
approximately 285,000
civilians then were living in the city,
and about 40,000 military were stationed there.
Of these, the number who died within four months
(when the acute illnesses subsided) was about
150,000, or slightly fewer:
in Hiroshima City Hall the number
is given as one hundred eighteen thousand.
There were many more — oh, countless more — who suffered
from exposure to the atomic bomb, and the effects
cover a very long period of time, including damage
to the unborn then and on the genes for generations
yet to come. Damage to the psyche ran
deeper — it can never be quantified —
and that full story too remains to be told.

❖ ❖ ❖ ❖ ❖ ❖

AT HIROSHIMA
The sun fell down red
flaming from the summer sky
lightning-melted

in the blacking rain
fear becomes a river but
then it had no name

40

O you autumn winds
can you tell me where to find
my particular Hell?

We *hibakusha**
have already suffered much
in burns, pains, and scars —
worse: immersed in death, numbed, we
must keep permanent death watch.

Hiroshima (the "wide island") on the Ota delta
where branches of the river were filled that fated day
with little white boats of paper and thin wood
on which deceased family names were inscribed:
memorials for the dead in the time of O-Bon
joined now by those who thirsted and were dying —
the river Ota clogged the O-Bon memorials
and the dying and the corpses of the dead

---

* *hibakusha*: atomic bomb survivors, including those who entered the affected areas too soon after the
bombing.

CANTO V

AT NAGASAKI

Human history becomes more and more
a race between education and catastrophe.
                    H. G. Wells, *Outline of History*

Hiroshima was in effect cut off from
the rest of the world, and the Japanese
government had limited information about
the effects of the bombing.

... Why was a second city attacked so quickly?
Why weren't the Japanese given additional time
to evaluate the results of the first bombing?
Was the decision-making process a serious
and thoughtful one?
                    Gar Alperovitz, *The Decision to*
                    Use the Atomic Bomb, 532

The military orders covered Hiroshima and
one further site:
> Additional bombs will be
> delivered on the above targets
> as soon as made ready by the project staff.
> — thus Acting Army Chief of Staff Handy,
> to the Commander of Strategic Air Forces
> in the Pacific, Spaatz, on July 25th.

The Japanese could not know that there were
only two atomic bombs made ready.
(General Groves held up shipment to the Pacific
of the Plutonium 239 core for
another bomb — otherwise a third bomb
would have been on hand at Tinian around
the 24th of August. This they could not have known.)

Three days after Hiroshima Nagasaki was fated.
This time plutonium was used to make
the bomb, which was dropped from a B-29
on August 9th, producing a blast
equal to 21,000 tons
of TNT, scientists calculated.
The now-familiar mushroom cloud was seen:
it towered some sixty thousand feet
into the sky, overtopping the clouds
and touching the very vaults of heaven.
It killed immediately a third of the pre-war
population — about 40,000 — injuring
another 25,000, and destroying or
seriously damaging two out of five
of the city's structures. More powerful
than the bomb dropped upon Hiroshima
(including those who died later that year,

the total numbered 73,000),
the terrain reduced destruction — that,
and the smaller size of Nagasaki.
There was a double irony in the place.
First, that it was a secondary target
taken only after Kokura was concealed
by clouds (Kokura Arsenal on the north
coast of Kyushu), but it was the place
where Mitsubishi torpedoes used at Pearl
Harbor had been made. Yet the center of
the downtown Nagasaki area was the target
that the bomb missed. Little consolation
in all this for victims, less for survivors
(the lucky ones, one historian writes,
"were those who were killed outright" — suffering
was a heavy price to pay for survival).

The second irony was that Nagasaki
long had been a Christian center in Japan:
the place where in the sixteenth century
the Portuguese traders had introduced
on one hand Roman Catholicism and
with the other hand the smiling traders
dealt in guns. The Catholic cathedral
overlooked the stark wasteland of despair.

❖ ❖ ❖ ❖ ❖ ❖

It is fitting and just that Nagasaki
now has a Peace Park on the Urakami-
gama — *established under the point of
the detonation of their bomb* — and that
it has significance for Japanese

as *a spiritual center for movements*
to ban nuclear weapons.
The largest
Roman Catholic church in the Far East at
Nagasaki's Urakami was destroyed
by the bomb but built again in 1959.
Nearby in 1962 a shrine
was built commemorating twenty-six
martyrs crucified there in 1597.

❖ ❖ ❖ ❖ ❖ ❖

Irony, ambiguity, and complexity
lie at the heart of every human story
and are rooted deeply in human soil.
History is not written in straight lines.

❖ ❖ ❖ ❖ ❖ ❖

REBIRTH

Through the deep cellar, where only shadows live,
Shadows of the living and the dead, a cry broke,
A cry of pain through darkness,
No cry of joy, yet a consolation,
Drowning the thousand other cries that still
Re-echo shrilly through their heads,
An answer comes. From among those shadows
'Cry as you will, woman,' comes the answer.
'I know the way. In such hours of heaviness
It was my daily task to be with you
Up there.'
And this too helped:
Thus, unseen, a new life came,

46

Born of darkness. Out of darkness
Into light, for surely he
Was destined for the light.
Yet those who helped him then,
The consolers and the helpers, might themselves
Never again see light. Before the first
Gleam could reach into their cellar, they
Had been forever snuffed, like candles.

      — Thus Sadako Kurihara in *Ghugoku Bunka*,
       a collection of poems in March 1946.

CANTO VI

CHILDREN AND THE UNBORN

The loss of even one human life or the mal-
formation of even one baby . . . should be
of concern to all of us.

> John F. Kennedy (address July 1963, announ-
> cing the end of U. S. atmospheric testing)

Whoever causes one of these little ones who
believe in me to sin, it would be better for him
if a great millstone were hung round his neck
and he were thrown into the sea.

> Mark 9: 42

Piccolo mondo, my Italian friend would say,
and Hiroshima has touched my life in a dozen ways.
The doctor who in 1949 was assigned
Physician-in-Charge of the U.S. Atomic
Bomb Casualty Commission in Nagasaki
was a Japanese-American whose family
were interned during the long hard years of war
in an Arkansas camp. Still more coincidentally,
Dr. James Yamazaki joined the 106th
Infantry Division in Atterbury, Indiana,
just as I was leaving it to go to hospital.
His book, *Children of the Atomic Bomb*,
is a moving memoir of his life and his
experiences in Nagasaki, Hiroshima,
and the post-war testing in the Marshall Islands.
"We must wait until twenty years, I think"
(wrote Yamazaki), "until the end of the normal
life span of the youngest survivors, before
we can know the full story of the effects
on those exposed to the radiation of the bombs.
No one can say how much longer it might take
for defects to show up in succeeding generations."

What do we know? Leukemia was the first
cancer diagnosed, then in the long run
breast cancer proved more prevalent — this where
the rate of breast cancer is one of the lowest
in the world. More harrowing is the flood
of abnormalities: *the immature,*
developing brain is far more vulnerable
to radiation than more mature brains,
thus the particular vulnerability
of the brain in the fetus. Brain lesions, further,
revealed *how radiation dismantles*

orderly layers of brain cells and scrambles
them into a tangled confusion of cells
of altered size. He tells of Mrs. Kondo's
daughter, a woman then of forty-five
with mental retardation, though she had borne
two children of her own who showed no symptoms —
there is no evidence of a genetic defect.
But Mrs. Kondo's daughter cannot function
normally, and she relates to her own
children more as a sister than a mother.
"Doctor" (Mrs. Kondo said to Yamazaki),
"we must protect each other. We must confront
it now for the sake of the future of
our children living in the Nuclear Age."

Among survivors the trauma still is raw,
and some could not continue interviews
because simply to return to those events
in memory is too emotionally
overwhelming. Pervasive among survivors
(Yamazaki summarizes) are these emotions:
a bitterness from feeling that it was not
necessary to bomb a populated city;
and there is here (as elsewhere with survivors)
intractable guilt for many who recall,
in panic of light, ignoring cries for help
from persons trapped in the rubble, caught under
collapsed walls, as fire spread through the shattered city.

Pain is incommensurable
    and suffering unendurable
unless there is a meaning or
    an end for which the two are borne.

Guilt sits heavily on those
who fled the burning stones,
and equally it sits on those
who left their comrades even
to be sent to hospital.
Time does not succeed in
anaesthetizing all our guilt,
and time itself we find
is an imperfect anodyne.

For those of us who carry on to live
years of pilgrimage lie still ahead:
    You have not done enough,
    the Secretary General wrote
    in private meditations:
    you have never done enough
    so long as it is still
    possible that you have
    something of value to contribute.
The burden of this uncertain answer
must serve to reward each day.

❖ ❖ ❖ ❖ ❖ ❖

We do well to hear the Indian prayer
quoted by Dr. Yamazaki in his book:

THE PEACEMAKER

Think not forever of yourselves, O Chiefs,
    Nor of your own generations.
Think of continuing generations of our families.
Think of our grandchildren and of those yet unborn,
Whose faces are coming from beneath the ground.
      — On the formation of the Iroquois
        Confederation many centuries ago

And we turn to songs from the children of the ashes:

THE SONGS OF THE CHILDREN

Children in Japan were given a song
to teach the basics of civil defence:
    Air raid! Air raid! Here comes an air raid!
    Red! Red! Incendiary bomb!
    Run! Run! Get mattress and sand!
    Air raid! Air raid! Here comes an air raid!
    Black! Black! Here come the bombs!
    Cover your ears! Cover your eyes!

Then the bomb came.
    It rains and rains,
    In the slanting rain I sit,
    It drums upon my singed eyebrows,
    It runs into that bleeding hole, my mouth.

    Rain on my wounded shoulders,
    Rain in my lacerated heart.
    Rain, rain, rain,
    Wherefore do I live on?

❖ ❖ ❖ ❖ ❖ ❖

And in the void and chaos afterward:
> *Not on the skin alone*
> *Suppurate pustules.*
> *Deeper are the heart wounds,*
> *Will they ever heal?*
>> — Kazuo's poem *Children of the Ashes*

CANTO VII

THE DOOMSDAY CLOCK:
SCIENTISTS AND OTHERS

In 1947 the doomsday clock first appeared
on the cover of the *Bulletin of the Atomic
Physicists* [founded in December 1945] as a
simple symbol of nuclear danger. In 1949
the magazine moved the minute hand to three
minutes before midnight to dramatize the ex-
plosion of its first atomic bomb by the
Soviet Union.

Humanity has yet to fully understand
the nuclear dangers.

> Len Ackland (*New York Times*,
> 3 December 1995)

Nuclear physicists formed their own
association and founded their own magazine,
The Bulletin of the Atomic Scientists,
which in May 1946 published
the Franck Report of the Chicago Atomic
Scientists that in June 1945
had strongly argued against a surprise attack
upon Japan and urged instead for demonstration
in some uninhabited area, but without
agreement on how or under what conditions
the military use of atom weapons
might be made. Charged with delivery of that
document to the White House, Arthur Compton
took a week to get the petition to Washington,
taking it to Grove's office, and there it passed
to Stimson — never, it seems, seen by the president.
It then took one year to achieve openness
on such a vital matter as this document.

> Things were in the saddle then, not
> open to or to be controlled by us,
> ordinary soldiers soon-to-be veterans,
> and events moved in the world at break-neck speed:
> war turned into victory and slid carelessly
> into Cold War, and we felt lapped by the new
> generation barking at our war-weary heels.
> That someone in the command chain sat on,
> then managed by whatever spuriously-
> assumed power successfully to quash
> so thoughtful and informed a document
> is outrageous in any democracy.

The matter is complex, and there are several kinds
of issues here involved, with many voices
(some clamoring at the time, others later added).
The loudest and most strident was the voice

of that senator from Wisconsin (whose house
I owned when later I lived on Capitol Hill):
the ultimate degeneration of a man
of politics, that feculent person
in the august U. S. Senate chamber
who did not know the meaning of conscience.
Not least and at great cost the ruffian stormed
the Senate and the media with his harsh
unsubstantiated charges until his
exposure in a Senate committee hearing
of which TV cameras (at the very dawn
of the new electronic age) gave the watching nation
an unforgettable image of blustering
and manipulation of the truth. Yes, he
and Nixon shared in muffling the voice
of Oppenheimer, who might otherwise
have added much to levels of public
discourse and civility discussing
public policy on atomic matters
in those murky frightened post-war years
when private conscience was a rare commodity.

❖ ❖ ❖ ❖ ❖ ❖

Memoirs and related literature poured forth
in post-war years, and nearly all concerned
tried to excuse or palliate their role
in the making and the decision to drop
the atomic bomb. Thus Truman as late
as 1966 told one journalist
(informed that Truman kept control of certain papers
in his Library at Independence, Missouri,
and regarded them as "his"), he planned not
to relinquish them "until I'm good and ready."

More honest and direct was Leahy's statement:

> *It is my opinion that the use of this*
> *barbarous weapon at Hiroshima and*
> *Nagasaki was of no material assistance*
> *in our war against Japan. The Japanese*
> *were already defeated and ready to*
> *surrender. My own feeling was that in being*
> *the first to use it, we had adopted an ethical*
> *standard common to the barbarians*
> *of the Dark Ages. I was not taught to make war*
> *in that fashion, and wars cannot be won*
> *by destroying women and children. ...*

Yet estimates were released of casualties
projected if there were to be invasion of
the Japanese heartland: these varied by
tens — even hundreds — of thousands. Careers
and reputations were on the line, they thought,
and journalists more interested in ratings
than in truth repeated or enlarged upon
the myth that the bomb was needed to prevent
or obviate invasion of Japan.
The U.S. Catholic bishops urged in '83,

> *we must shape the climate of opinion which*
> *will make it possible for our country*
> *to express profound sorrow over the atomic*
> *bombings in 1945. Without that sorrow*
> *there is no possibility of finding a way*
> *to repudiate future use of nuclear weapons.*

❖ ❖ ❖ ❖ ❖ ❖

Have we not learned that Vietnam also taught
> *that even the best leaders will lie to their people*
> *about the most fundamental issues if they*

are not constrained by effective checks and balances?
Without openness — which certainly one might
expect after a fifty-year silence —
Alperovitz concludes, *there can be no*
democratic responsibility: indeed,
without accountability, there can be
no continuity of democracy.

❖ ❖ ❖ ❖ ❖ ❖

In 1946 there could have been a turning-point:
the war was over, and it was time for writing history.
That year Churchill told Mountbatten,
> *The decision to release the atom bomb*
> *was perhaps the only thing which history*
> *will have serious questions about* (and added)
> *I may even be asked by my Maker why*
> *I used it, but I shall defend myself*
> *vigorously and say, 'Why did you release*
> *this knowledge to us when mankind was raging*
> *in furious battles?'*
And to George Bernard Shaw
he wrote in August 1946,
> *Do you think that the atomic bomb means*
> *that the architect of the universe got tired*
> *of writing his non-stop scenario? There was*
> *a lot to be said for his stopping with the Panda.*
> *The release of the bomb seems to be his next turning-*
> *point...*

❖ ❖ ❖ ❖ ❖ ❖

The questions about the dropping of the bomb
enlarged with H-bomb testings in the Pacific

and Nevada, and reports of devastation
of the plant and human life on scattered atolls;
and we began to worry about the long-range effects
of nuclear bombs, and even nuclear energy.

Just as physical effects of radiation
may take years to manifest themselves, so
the mind responds in different ways over
the years: some response going on in individuals,
some reaction taking place in groups. Thus
there was the atmosphere of Pugwash ten years
later, in 1957, reacting
to the Bikini H-bomb tests. There was
the world of Bertrand Russell and his campaign
for Nuclear Disarmament. And students
everywhere often lost all hope for their future.

Nuclear Discussion among Students
    To sit and hear the talk
    of world catastrophe
    from young lips and to see
    the bitterness in eyes
    still bright with joy of life
    is Atomwinter dark
    and cyanide-like cold
    deep in my keening heart.
My generation had destroyed much in
the spiritual life of the young, not planting
enough substantial to grow in its place.
There were — as I taught literature, I thought —
these ways to make response.

1. *As from a future Greek Anthology*

> there is a shuffling of sandals
> and odours of unguents and oils
> to celebrate the new barbarians
> born outside the ruined chips and coils
> of burned-out cities lit now by candles
> in the cold aftermath of nuclear
> meltdown. Regardless of all they say:
> *Timor mortis conturbat me.*

2. *As from a medieval lyric*

> The fear of death confounds me
> the fear of all beyond surrounds me
> the fear of dying so impounds me ...

3. *Theatrum mundi*

> NOTICE
> this theatre will be closed
> for an indefinite time.

4. *A New Poem from the Old Persian*

> naked we came out of the dark
> naked again we must return
> after the explosion in the park
> naked again
>   after we burn

5. *Epitaph (after Rexroth)*

Fire on fire in fire of fire
we shall consume and be consumed
by fire
            and be entombed.

❖ ❖ ❖ ❖ ❖ ❖

Ten years ago Chernobyl let us know
that danger lurked in the nuclear plants
and that disaster spreads upon the winds.

The making of atomic bombs in China,
India, and Pakistan, perhaps Libya,
gives reason to lose sleep at night, but some
will sleep through every danger and disaster.

❖ ❖ ❖ ❖ ❖ ❖

Again, the matter is complex with several
issues here involved, with many voices.
McCarthy proved Acton right in saying
*Power tends to corrupt, and absolute
power corrupts absolutely* — now, as then.

CANTO VIII

MEMORY, HERITAGE, AND CRISIS

Let every person be subject to
the governing authorities.
                    Paul, *Epistle to the Romans* 13: 1

... I thought it important from the Christian
standpoint to admit the moral ambiguity of
all righteous people in history. ...
                    Reinhold Niebuhr, Letter to J.B. Conant (1946)

History provides neither compensation for
suffering nor penalties for wrong.
                    Lord Acton, letter to Mandell Creighton (1887)

History is a tangled skein that one may take up
at any point, and break when one has unravelled
enough.
                    Henry Adams, *Education of Henry Adams*

[Moltke] had risen above the pettiness and
primitivism of latter-day nationalism.
                    George F. Kennan, *Memoirs*

Agreed: you cannot make the dead to walk,
O veteran, nor graveyard stones to talk —
and certainly not you nor I will try
to overturn old certitudes and make
a proud reversal of the values known
for centuries — we will not make right wrong.

But let's agree also that there will be
more than two sides to complex questions where
just black and white are too simplistic: *there*
the painter wants some color, or a touch of grey —
like Montaigne let us make further room
for a new distant thought, the third approach
that offers balancing of scales, perspective
from binocular vision now held in mind's
perspective-gaining hand.
                    Let irony
suggest how provisional is human fate,
let it adjudicate the black and white.

❖ ❖ ❖ ❖ ❖ ❖

Within the framework of the century
of war in every part of earth this
atomic bomb dropped on Hiroshima
is not quantitatively significant:
a hundred thousand dead, more or less,
against the megadeaths since 1914,
which according to Brzezinski recently
total one hundred ninety-seven million,
or ten percent of the world's total population
in 1900. Our civilization,
so-called, has had a predilection for war.

But statisticians do not tell us all,
and we must believe that wisdom is far
better than weapons of war. But with Job
we must press further: where shall wisdom be found?
and where is the place of understanding?

❖ ❖ ❖ ❖ ❖ ❖

Last year, attending a reunion of
the 106th Infantry Division,
I wrote this poem to an old comrade
(older than I, he has died before me):

>We had a common enemy
>*Then ... there ...* fifty years ago,
>and we were quick of step and strong
>of hand, and confidently so.
>
>In these men that I see today
>I look to recognize the bright
>eyes that I knew then, to find
>the comrades so long out of sight.
>
>We all have faced another foe,
>the marching unrelenting years,
>and we have tried to hold our ground
>against the losses and the fears.

Fear is a constant: physical in time of war,
mental as we steadily grow older; and
spiritual as unreadily we face
the imminent reality of death.

But there are further constants we must face:
old questions of authority and power,
and individual responsibility,
the role of conscience, and making allowance
for deeper experience and understanding
always potential in living with open mind —

>*Have you learned lessons only of those who*
>*admired you, and were tender with you, and*
>*stood aside for you? Have you not learned*
>*great lessons from those who reject you,*
>*and brace themselves against you? or who*
>*treat you with contempt, or dispute the passage*
>*with you?* (thus Walt Whitman in *Leaves of Grass*)

Now, thinking of the sibling bombs dropped
half a century ago, are we capable
of thinking something like *Hosannah ex infernis?*
and beyond thought, to pray — aware that prayers
in time of war to the same God for victory
become ironic exercises (become,
or *seem?*)? Where and by whom during war years
was this verse sung,

>*If together we cling*
>*singing God save the King*
>*and throw men overboard to the sharks...*

Should we teach children other verses to
Onward Christian Soldiers — should we, that is,
continue viewing life as war, each one a soldier?

Fear may be a necessary condition:
Sallust in his history of Roman wars
had this to say:

>*Before the destruction of Carthage*
>*the Roman people and Senate together*
>*governed the commonwealth peacefully*

and moderately, nor was there rivalry
among citizens for glory and power;
it was fear of the enemy that kept
the state on the path of justice.

(note that Sallust speaks of the people and the senate
governing together)

But when the minds
were freed from that fear, immorality and
arrogance, which are encouraged by prosperity,
entered them. Thus the peace which they had
desired proved all the more cruel and harsh
after they got it. For the nobles began
to turn their dignity, and the people their
liberty, into license, and every man took,
robbed, and pillaged for himself.

Are we Americans in fact a version
for the twentieth-century of Romans?

❖ ❖ ❖ ❖ ❖ ❖

Again, as many times before, I return
to Berdyaev's profound insight:

Eschatology is not an invitation to escape
into a private heaven: it is a call to
transfigure the evil and stricken world.
It is a witness to the end of the world
of ours with its enslaving objectifications....

If it is so difficult to govern
a commonwealth, need we marvel at the problems
in founding world order? The principle is
at least as old as Cicero: we must conceive
of this whole world as one commonwealth of which
both gods and men are to be valued. We are not alone.

TO AMERICAN STUDENTS TODAY

To have lost the war against a Hitler and
the Japanese war-mad military
would be unthinkable. One must go to war
to defend, and one must fight to win.

But: *power tends to corrupt*, the learned Acton
asserted — not the first to point this out,
but none have said it so succinctly —
and then he added: *absolute power corrupts absolutely.*
In any power structure this is true:
a fortiori of the military and the church,
but also in the university.
I have seen corruption in the corridors
of power of Army, Church, and university:
it is a subtle, quickly spreading thing.
A democracy especially must guard against
power abuses; there must be some accountability:
open communication (except in time of war)
with freedom to dissent is *the only true*
safeguard against popular corruption.

Students in universities are taught
(or should be taught, I say with Socrates)
to question what their masters say; soldiers
in uniform are taught they must perform
immediately with willing and unquestioning
obedience (and even cheerfully);
and members of a church have preached to them
injunctions of tradition-sanctioned institutions —
how do the young learn to distinguish?

A blocking-back in football I learned young
about subordinating individuality
to greater good of team, and in the army
I was taught the binding force of uniform
and that I must obey orders immediately
and cheerfully, and unquestioningly.
And, as a member of a Christian church I
read, and listen, and attempt to lead a life
not merely moral but even Christlike, with
the guidelines of the Bible, reason, and
the reinforcing sense of tradition —
the consensus of long generations of
teachers and preachers, saints and scholars —
here too there cannot be too much emphasis
on novelty, upon extravances of mind or will.
In institutions there must be always
accountability, a following of what
we called chain of command — that in the spheres
of principles, action and ideas work both
downwards from the leader and also upwards
from the lowest element in the chain,
a living tree of leafs, stem and roots.

❖ ❖ ❖ ❖ ❖ ❖

A LETTER TO A JAPANESE FRIEND

Your letter last year to *The Spectator*
entitled 'Soviet perfidy' spoke of
the more than five hundred thousand Japanese
soldiers and civilians illegally detained
(have we forgotten thousands of American
soldiers who disappeared into the Soviet
liberation army?), and I mark your point

that it was the declaration of war by
the Soviets, more than the Atom Bomb,
that led the Suzuki cabinet to accept
the terms of surrender — and there is more
for us to discuss, Akio, if you come
back to the States, or I should take the first step
in my long-anticipated journey to Japan.
And not until this year has there been movement
towards apology, or even recognition
of events before and during World War II:
on TV during August I saw the Mayor
of Hiroshima say that it was time
to apologize for Japanese atrocities.
We need to be reminded that the Japanese
had their own propaganda machine, proclaiming
in late October 1944
that it has gradually become clear that
the American enemy, driven by
its ambition to conquer the world, is coming
to attack us ... the barbaric tribe of
Americans are devils in human skin ...
Western Barbarian Demons ...
                          Thus it was
easy then to order Japanese military
to fight to the death and not consider surrender:
some did for weeks, and even years.
Yet we, on our part, must recognize the crimes of rape
committed by our servicemen in Okinawa
and Japan, and make apology for them
(apology must be the threshold of reparation).
And, going back to dropping of the bomb,
we surely now may question Edgar Guest's
infinitude of certitude faith-wrapped:

The power to blow all things to dust
Was kept for people God could trust,
And granted unto them alone
That evil might be overthrown.

Last year the Smithsonian in Washington
planned a 50th anniversary exhibit
of the *Enola Gay* and — no matter
the merits of that exhibit — there was
an outcry, a rush of censorship almost
beyond credibility. The commander
of the American Legion wrote:

> *We will insist that no materials*
> *related to the exhibit that is now*
> *canceled will be disseminated. We*
> *understand that the Institution*
> *will not produce such materials,*
> *and we will hold them to that promise.*

Such blatant censorship itself must be censored,
for this debacle was a shame for those who think.
Wrote Edward Linenthal, of the Smithsonian's
Exhibition Advisory Board:

> *In the end, we have all lost a great deal.*
> *We have lost a chance to offer a commemorative*
> *thanks to veterans. We have lost the chance*
> *to remind each other that irony, ambiguity,*
> *and complexity are part of every human story.*
> *And we have allowed the arrogance and igno-*
> *rance of members of Congress — acting as if*
> *they were commissars in a totalitarian state —*
> *to threaten a public institution, in effect,*
> *to press for the regulation of public memory.*

Historians (and the informed public) must
confront the past and search beyond the lies
and half-truths of a half-century ago.
(We torture ourselves over the future as well

as over the past, wrote Seneca a millennium ago.)
The dropping of the bomb on Hiroshima
can be justified in purely military terms:
>   *To avert a vast, indefinite butchery,*
wrote Winston Churchill in his history,
>   *to bring the war to an end, to give peace*
>   *to the world, to lay healing hands upon*
>   *its tortured peoples by a manifestation*
>   *of overwhelming power at the cost of a few*
>   *explosions*
(what a glossing over rhetoric can give
to agonies of suffering in that city!)
>   *seemed,*
>   *after all our toils and perils, a miracle*
>   *of deliverance.*

A miracle of deliverance Hiroshima
was to Allied forces, and in military terms
it has been justified, although the strict
moralist condemns choosing to kill the innocent
as a means to ends, as murder. Besides, can anyone
declare that Hiroshima was a purely military
target? Also—
>   *There was a gap,* as Marshall noted:
>   *What we did not take account was that*
>   *the destruction would be so complete that*
>   *it would be an appreciable time before*
>   *the actual facts of the case would get*
>   *to Tokyo. The destruction of Hiroshima*
>   *was so complete that there was no communication*
>   *at least for a day, I think, and maybe longer.*
In light of that stubborn fact, the bombing
only three days later of Nagasaki
cannot be condoned. No wonder Truman said the thought

of wiping out another hundred thousand was too horrible.
Meanwhile there was disputing of the terms
of surrender: Japanese took it that abdication
by the Emperor was being called for,
when after all he was allowed to stay.
And Russia entered into the Asian war
theatre, declaring war on 8 August.
You write, my friend, to tell me of your father,
the Ambassador's disclosure that it was
Russian entry that finally led
the government of Japan to surrender.
Our Admiral Leahy thought the submarines
had already cut the vital line supplying
mainland Japan with the necessary oil and food.
Can one speak so definitively about
a single cause of American victory?

You may not have read the final words
of Oppenheimer on leaving Los Alamos
on October 16, 1945 —
with history's hindsight they now seem prophetic:
> *The peoples of the world must unite,*
> *or they will perish. This war, that has ravaged*
> *so much of the earth, has written these words.*
> *The atomic bomb has spelled them out for all men*
> *to understand. Other men had spoken them,*
> *in other times, of other wars, of other weapons.*
> *They have not prevailed. There are some,*
> *misled by a false sense of human history,*
> *who hold that they will not prevail today.*
> *It is not for us to believe that. By our works*
> *we are committed, committed to a world united,*
> *before the common peril, in law, and in humanity.*

We surely are agreed, my friend, separated
by seven thousand miles of space, but not of thought
or sharing of deeply human values.

❖ ❖ ❖ ❖ ❖ ❖

DISCUSSION WITH A VETERAN OF THREE WARS

"Go back," I say, "to Eisenhower's Farewell
Address, and his wise words that warn us that
the potential for the disastrous rise
of misplaced power exists and will persist."
I do not think of this American general
as a prophet, but he led well and at the end
he spoke with clear mind and honestly.

I want you some day to read the letters
by Moltke to Freya, his wife. This German
our George Kennan called "the greatest person
morally, and the largest and most enlightened
in his concepts that I met on either side
of the battle-lines in the Second World War."
He was to Kennan over the years "a pillar
of moral conscience and unfailing source
of political and intellectual
inspiration" (we must have benchmarks, way-markings).
"The Apocalyptic Horsemen were beginners,"
Moltke wrote; and one day, reading the latest
gruesome news in Germany, "How can anyone
know these things and still walk around free?"
Conscience for him was clear, alive and strong,
and he was executed not long before
liberation of the camps and prisons: but
he was already free in spirit. That

Nazi Germany was the enemy
of all such men is clear, and to lose the war
against a Hitler or the Japanese
would be, again, unthinkable. Are we
agreed in this reasoning, my friend?

❖ ❖ ❖ ❖ ❖ ❖

DISCUSSIONS WITH MY EUROPEAN STUDENTS

But what is it that we must defend?
It cannot only be material things
and territory (though that may be legitimate).

Gabriel Marcel, philosopher, declared,
> *Today the first and perhaps the only duty*
> *of the philosopher is to defend man*
> *against himself: to defend man against*
> *that extraordinary temptation toward*
> *inhumanity to which — almost without*
> *being aware of it — so many human beings*
> *today have yielded. That inhumanity*
> *is possible in peace, but war gives it*
> *excuses, temptations, opportunities.*

Reflect the words of Berdyaev, just voiced,
that eschatology is not an invitation
to escape... But Berdyaev's philosophy
for some will not appear to come to grips
with the nitty-gritty of *Realpolitik*
(the pragmatic politics of a Kissinger).
Are we agreed, fellow students (for such we be)
that the principle of a just war still remains,
but that application in a concrete case

can come only after careful consideration?
Even the language of the law ranges from *casus
belli*, an occasion for war or an act
regarded as justifying war, to *casus
fortuitus*, an accident, and *casus
omissus*, a case not provided for in law.
To speak of justice we must first
be just, and absolute in accuracy.

❖ ❖ ❖ ❖ ❖ ❖

To All My Friends

"The end is not yet": Christian contemplation
(I cannot speak for Buddhist or Shinto)
must make allowance for continuing
revelation — we may soon understand
more than we were able to do yesterday.
Yet: the world never learns, it seems, about
the cost of war. *History has a way
of making the past palatable, the dead
a dream*, the poet Richard Hugo wrote.
We build distances from the aching past,
otherwise we could not face the reality,
the horror and the pain, or even the sheer
boredom.
                    War is ancient, universal,
and as up-to-date as today, Americans
learned from their TVs during Desert Storm
(and some of it as hyped as any hard-
pitched advertising commercial spots).
Ultimately — and some time in life we all
must face the ultimate (but on earth we find
the Ultima Thule tends to be tied to things,

to market values of a person's life,
and on earth the true Ultima Thule recedes
and the spiritual ultimate is a goal
that not only do we not reach, we lose sight of).
It depends not so much upon man's will
or exertion as upon God's mercy. Knowing that,
we can accept today and bravely face tomorrow:
we have tomorrow bright before us like a flame.

The fourteenth-century English mystic Julian
of Norwich saw the whole Godhead concentrated
as it were in a single point. And in that fated place,
and on that fateful date, the whole of existence,
focused on the Hiroshima epicenter.
How many there, that day, knew God is the fine point
without magnitude which is the deep center
of the human heart?

                              If it be true, as Julian
said, that
                    Sin is Behovely, but
                    All shall be well, and
                    All manner of things shall be well,
the path is clear, but it is not a simple one,
the way is hard. Whatever I might say about their pain
(those thousands surviving at Hiroshima
and Nagasaki) would be quite inadequate:
their pain is greater far than I could
possibly imagine: pain of flesh and body,
anguish of spirit, loss of hope and joy.
Yet the higher and greater and sweeter our love
so much the deeper will be our sorrow when
we see the bodies of those suffering —

How much the world's Divine Maker
must have suffered on this day,
how much He must still suffer
over pain inflicted on our fellow men,
those who do not turn away, nor do they all
reject God's Providence.
                 The bomb descending broke the air
                 above Hiroshima in one great flame
                 of incandescent terror ...
It was the intersection of the timeless moment
for those countless thousands at that place — they
had to know, to learn, the only hope or else
despair,
                 Lies in the choice of pyre or pyre —
                 to be redeemed with fire by fire.
If Sin be necessary, with Julian we learn
that pain caused by sin is something lasting only
a little while: it purges us and makes us know
ourselves, so that we ask for mercy.
                 I marvel
at those survivors who now bear no hatred
towards the countrymen of bombers who inflicted pain
(would we, had we been in their stead now feel the same?).
Instead they manifest a love excusing us
and overlooking blame. In place of laying blame
they have made a new beginning, born with the dead,
and so for them life finds a different path
learning to live in another pattern
different from what they learned from the past.
For them, for us, the way of liberation
leads through the present towards the future.
Beyond fear and dying there is a land
of living, for what lies beyond dying is not death.

EPILOGUE

The Journeying of the Mind to God

One road alone does not suffice to
attain so great a mystery!
> Symmachus. *Report on The Altar of Victory, 10*

Today a Babylonian confusion and fragmentation
prevails. ... For when the desperate violence of
the world will have made every man a Cain,
the words of St. Paul will resound once more —
those words which alone are sacred and eternal:
peace, love, mercy, justice — in the spirit
which is the Lord.
> Ernesto Buonaiuti in *The Mystic Vision* (1970)

What madness not to understand how to love
human beings with awareness of the human condition!
> St. Augustine, *Confessions*

... already my desire and my will were turned
like a wheel that is evenly moved by the Love
that moves the sun and other stars.
> Dante, *Paradiso* xxxiii

The meaning of all lives lies in the living,
not in abstractions of philosophy
or even formulations of theology,
and living is a series of journeyings
from one stage to the next, from one level
of understanding to another. Standing still
is rusting one's deep capabilities —
even well-oiled finely-tuned mechanisms
of monastic conscience rust.
                              It is easy to hate,
too easy to seek revenge in great or small,
but that way costs the one who gives himself
to hate more than the target of the hating.
Violations of any code or contract
or of a treaty lead to retribution, thus
to revenge and retaliation, and
there is no ending to this chain of hate,
this cycle of repeated acts of hatred.
There is no profit and no end to hating.

But merely to tolerate is not to reconcile.
We move, we must go further, in the learning
that revenge leads always to reciprocal revenge.
The repeated patterns of hate must stop
here in the presentiment of time.
                              Know
the process is agonizingly slow,
and there are never any shortcuts.
One cannot sustain a march or climb
without that precious commodity, humility.
                    In each phrase and line of poetry
                    (wrote Paz) there is concealed
                    the possibility of failure:

the poet too must press on
and risk in order to succeed.

❖ ❖ ❖ ❖ ❖ ❖

After five years I was ready to shed
my proud Army uniform, with jump boots,
and to begin my Princeton *vita nuova* — my
apprenticeship to scholarship — that led
to twelve years at Cornell and Notre Dame.
I stumbled (God knows) often enough, but the road
led on; I made the border crossing to
Toronto, there learned greatly in St. Mike's
and the Mediaeval Institute. The route
was Augustinian, through Thomas and
Erasmus. Invitations came unsought:
I went to Washington, launching the Folger
Institute, saw politicians hard at work
politicking and staff officers too far removed
from command. Experience was wide and deep,
the pace at times was frantic, and at times
I lost the path (I left Dominican
certitude) and wandered. But I moved on
in my own journey of the mind. Slowly
I have turned, as communities of men
must turn, to understanding of the other side —
the Other — that must be part of any
negotiations of business, spirit or mind.
To forgive does not mean to forget: we
have always that luxury of the usury-prone
temperament of man. The *itinerarium,*
the travelling of the mind towards God,
is an itinerary available, and necessary, for every man.
Bonded, as it must be, as part of being

and the beginning to know thyself:
just as iron sharpens iron, so knowing oneself
(a lengthy process, which Wordsworth thought
the prelude to a fuller excursion) so knowing
oneself sharpens awareness of the journey that
one begins at birth and ends only with death.
One cannot waste a day of that long journeying,
and we must reach out in dialoguing.

Towards Dialogue

Behind Oppenheimer, he who guided theory
at the Los Alamos lab and led
to creation of the intricate mechanism
of the first atomic bomb, we hear the words
of Emerson (from his 1842 Journals):
> *The tongue of flame ... the volcano also,*
> *from which the conflagration rises towards*
> *the zenith ... A spark of fire is infinitely*
> *deep, but a mass of fire reaching from the earth*
> *upward into heaven, this is the sign of*
> *the robust, united, burning, radiant soul.*

"Yes, our days demand fire, and in this damning
epoch-making war we had to have a rising fire."

From Moltke, that man of moral greatness, hear:
> *Be subject to the higher powers put over you —*
> *but only until one's own integrity and moral*
> *conscience obligates us to stand up in opposition.*

And he, had he been given life after the war, might
say to Oppenheimer:
> To you, who studied in my Germany
> before the coming of the Hitler menace,
> let me repeat my words of 1940:

Freedom and natural order are the necessary
poles that dictate where statecraft must move.
A human being can be free only in
the framework of the natural order, and
an order is natural only if it leaves man free."
We must agree on these, I think. And you and I
who have gone through our private hells (but you
spent your last months in Nazi prison) agree,
bearing the proud Prussian name *von Moltke*
you led an anti-Hitler Resistance group
and died in January 1945
leaving as legacy *Letters to Freya.*

> *When thou pass through the waters,*
> *I will be with thee; and through the rivers,*
> *they shall not overflow thee; when thou*
> *walkest through the fire, thou shalt not be burned;*
> *neither shall the flame kindle upon thee.*
> (Isaiah 43).

And for after the war, the rest of Isaiah's prophecy,
> *Let all the nations gather together,*
> *and let the peoples assemble.*

❖ ❖ ❖ ❖ ❖ ❖

And to these two, let us bring forth the spirit
of one who guided the U.N. towards peace,
who wrote,
> *You have not done enough, you have never*
> *done enough, so long as it is still*
> *possible that you have something of value*
> *to contribute.*
> (Hammarskjöld, *Markings*)

83

The shaper and director of the U.N. declared

> *So shall the world be created each morning anew,*
> *forgiven — in Thee, by Thee.*

Would he not say to Oppenheimer (as he said to himself),

> *Do not look back. And do not dream about*
> *the future, either. It will neither give you back*
> *the past, nor satisfy your other daydreams.*
> *Your duty, your reward — your destiny —*
> *are* here *and* now.

And to von Moltke might he not have said,

> *Courage and love: equivalent and related*
> *expressions of your bargain with Life. You*
> *are willing to 'pay' what your heart commands*
> *you to give. Two associated reflexes*
> *to the sacrificial act, conditioned by*
> *a self-chosen effacement of the personality*
> *in the One. One result of 'God's marriage*
> *to the Soul' is a union with other people*
> *which does not draw back before the ultimate*
> *surrender of the self.*
>
> (*Markings*)

All three knew, each in his own terms, the fullness
of the surrender of the self. The force of fire
lay at the core of each man's cosmology,
and for each the heart of eschatology was love.

❖ ❖ ❖ ❖ ❖ ❖

Yeats in old age was voicing conscience
for my generation when he wrote that
"I think it better that in times like these
a poet's mouth be silent, for in truth
we have no gift to set a statesman right."

> ('On Being Asked for a War Poem')

The decades since that war have telescoped
> *(times are not empty: nor do they idly go*
> *and roll through our senses with no effect on us,*
> Augustine meditates in his *Confessions)*
and I discover new meaning in old tropes,
and thus a psalm is offered for our times:

A Psalm For Our Times

Who will be blamed,
> who cursed for inhumanity?
How can we not weep when we look upon the children?
> What can we say to them when they ask why?
It is not only politicians who lie;
> the generals have been known to lie to protect
> their record, their part in the decision.
It is we who must look to the future for hope.
> It is always the future that we prepare
> the ground for, and for which we seed.
We cannot hope to know all the truth,
> and even partial truths come only in the
> goodness of time.
We must believe that something happened here
> that is worth remembering;
> We must believe that something is left worth saving.
Make me hear of joy and gladness,
> *that the bones you have broken may rejoice.*
We must strengthen both our hope and our patience.
> We must be willing to redeem the past by what we do
> and what we become as we grow older.
The answer is love;
> the way is loving.

A NOTE ON THE FORM, PROSODY, AND TITLE OF THE POEM

An epic can most simply be defined as a long narrative poem, typically distinguished from other narratives by its greater length and its focussing on a single heroic figure or event, and told in an elevated tone or manner (the grand style of the rhetoricians and poets). The mythic or legendary achievement that is portrayed in great detail has characteristically been one that is central to the traditions and beliefs of its culture — whether Homer's *Iliad* and *Odyssey*, or Virgil's *Aeneid*, or *Beowulf*, or Dante's *Inferno*. The making and dropping of an atomic bomb upon Hiroshima and Nagasaki is manifestly such an event, and it is one that subsumes the traditions and beliefs — and anxieties — of American culture.

In the long history of the epic there has been a remarkable continuity of conventions: the episodic structure, the beginning in the middle of things (*in medias res*), a formal invocation (more often than not linked with the sublime style), extended similes, elaborated descriptions of weapons and armor (like the celebrated making of Achilles' shield). The epic form has often incorporated lyric and dramatic elements along with the narrative. In the nineteenth century two developments greatly enlarged the epic: Goethe in his *Faust* evolved a form that is epic in its thrust but essentially dramatic in its form; and Wagner, especially in his *Ring of the Nibelungen*, created a fusion of musical and dramatic form.

In *My Hiroshima* I have endeavored to write the story of the bombing of Hiroshima as an epic, while construing the genre as multi-faceted and demanding many voices, as well as introducing various lyric forms. I have drawn upon my own personal experience (sometimes simply contemporaneous, but always, I trust, at least thematically relevant) in order to add one further thread of unity to the poem.

In English poetry, blank verse is largely the creation of the Renaissance, where it served the purpose of dramatic verse for Shakespeare and others, and of epic verse for Milton and others. Under the right persuasion, blank verse offers flexibility and a greater approximation to speech rhythms than rhymed and a highly patterned verse are likely to do. Within the larger commitment to blank verse in the poem, there is the possibility of internal rhyme, as well as employments of assonance and alliteration, and these techniques may serve to knit together verse-passages or to carry special emphasis, as well as to avoid the possibility of too many lines that are too regularly iambic pentameter, even when unrhymed. There are many short lines, as well as lines with extra syllables and feet — the models change. At times the rhythm shifts to that of spoken prose, with perhaps at times the tone of the classroom lecturer. More obviously, there are the interspersed lyric moments whose purpose should be self-evident.

Implicitly the poet is always a part of his poem: not even Homer or Virgil or Milton was able to distance himself completely from his work, and in our post-modern world we are likely to stress the role or presence of the poet much more than earlier generations would have done. I have called my poem *My Hiroshima* in part for this reason: the poem is about my experiencing (or not experiencing) the grim realities of that event, and my attempting long after the fact to understand it; and the title recognizes that there is a personal perspective which I consciously project. It may be a limitation of the poem but, if so, it is one that I accept.

There is another reason for the title. For so global an event — in its initial historical dimensions, and still more for its consequences and meanings — there must be more than one portraying, accounting, evaluation. I cannot pretend to speak for an entire generation of Americans who were young and in uniform in August 1945; yet my account, as honest and full as I can make it, may shed light for subsequent generations.

The poem, therefore, is *My Hiroshima.*

R.J.S.

1945-1997

A GUIDE TO THE SOURCES

The primary and secondary literature on the building and dropping of the atomic bomb are now almost impossibly large and diverse, and I cannot pretend to have read a major part of that bulk. Further, that scope and magnitude are made more complex by the fact that my reading of books and articles on Hiroshima has been done over a period of many years, making precise citation or attribution most difficult, and making it impossible to identify precisely my thinking at a particular time. Yet Lifton and Mitchell begin their 1995 book with the warning that "you cannot understand the twentieth century without Hiroshima": one must begin somewhere, however late, or piecemeal, or however much built on the shifting sands of memory.

There are the official publications and the memoirs. A most useful book has been that of Herbert Feis, *Japan Subdued: The Atomic Bomb and the End of the War in the Pacific*, which appeared in 1961 and its republication in 1966 under the title *The Atomic Bomb and the End of World War II* incorporates a number of subtle revisions that help chart shifts of opinion even from 1961 to 1966. Next there is the powerful argument of Gar Alperovitz in *The Decision to Use the Atomic Bomb* (1995), so rich in its citation of primary material (especially archival sources); it is a controversial argument, yet it is exhaustively documented and strongly argued, and it cannot be ignored. In *Hiroshima in America: Fifty Years of Denial*, Robert Jay Lifton and Greg Mitchell (1995) present an analysis of official distortions of information about the bombing, and then offer a probing of "Hiroshima's Legacy": the moral, psychological, and political implication of what has been lost by not facing the truth concerning Hiroshima. There is no doubt: "Hiroshima remains a raw nerve," and the cancelling of the so-called *Enola Gay* Exhibit at the Smithsonian on January 30, 1995, was in effect an act of censorship: see further *Judgement at the Smithsonian*, edited by Philip Nobile (1995).

William L. Laurence's contemporary account of the dropping of the bomb, in *Dawn Over Zero* (1947), remains a graphic narrative of the development and dropping of the bomb; and his narrative is reinforced by Leslie R. Grove's *Now It Can Be Told* (1963). One may follow the story of developing reflections about the bomb and its consequences and responsibilities in *Hiroshima Plus 20* (1965); and Richard Rhode's prize-winning *The Making Of the Atomic Bomb* (1986) is most thoroughly documented with clearcut portrayals of the scientific, political, and military figures involved. (For putting American generals and admirals in the larger context of worldwide military leadership one may profitably turn to *Who's Who in Military History*, edited by John Keegan and Andrew Wheatcroft, 1996, as well as to Keegan's excellent studies of leadership, especially *The Mask of Command*, 1987.)

There are numerous accounts of the days immediately following the bombing — I have not reread John Hersey's memorable *Hiroshima* since it appeared in *The*

New Yorker more than fifty years ago, recalling the shocking experiencing of his story of six people who lived through the explosion, but not wanting to be too much influenced in writing my own account. One might begin, as I did a year ago, with *Hiroshima Diary: The Journal of a Japanese Physician, August 6 — September 30, 1945*, by Michiko Hachia (1995). To that should be added the memoir of James N. Yamazaki, *Children of the Atomic Bomb* (1995) — with the added interest for me that Yamazaki had been a surgeon in the 106th Infantry Division in Europe. *The Children of Hiroshima*, complied by Dr. Arata Osada (1982) and *Widows of Hiroshima*, edited by Mikio Kanda (1989), together with the volume that combined the text of Betty Jean Lifton with the photographs by Eikoh Josoe — *A Place Called Hiroshima* (1985) — are all powerful testimonies by survivors.

Questions about the dropping of the atomic bomb — that is the necessity for and the rightness of the decisions — inevitably lead to fuller discussions of the morality of nuclear warfare. The earlier books of this poem have tried to maintain the civilian and enlisted man's perspectives of pre-1945, when the writer had neither been informed about the Manhattan Project nor had the luxury of time to think about the implications of nuclear warfare: the later books of this poem have very much a post-1945 perspective. I cite here some publications which influenced my own thinking, during the 1970s and 1980s, especially. The several writings of Barbara Ward were a strong influence upon my increasingly international bent of thought, especially her *Nationalism and Ideology* (1966). Note should be made of these two academic studies: *Justice and War in the Nuclear Age*, edited by Robert R. Reilly et al. (1983); and James P. Sterba, *The Ethics of War and Nuclear Deterrence* (1985), which includes the eloquent essay by George F. Kennan that cries out against the use of nuclear weapons against other human beings as "nothing less than a presumption, a blasphemy, an indignity — an indignity of monstrous dimensions — offered to God!" (In the late 1950s I had become an assistant to the editor of the *American Journal of Jurisprudence*, and remained on the editorial board until 1996: this experience enriched the soil of my thinking.) Robert F. Rizzo's "Nuclear War: the Moral Dilemma," in *Cross Currents* xxxii (1982) provides a useful summary of some discussion of the 1960s and 1970s.

Reaction to the dropping of the bombs, and reactions to the questions raised, have been widespread and longlasting. In their book on *Hiroshima in America*, Lifton and Mitchell include an appendix "Cultural Response to Hiroshima," which surveys the portrayal of Hiroshima's bombing on film and in fiction and poetry. An anthology of more than a hundred poems about nuclear war and disaster — many dealing with Hiroshima — was published in 1995, *Atomic Ghosts*. Earlier, Marc Kaminsky (in a cycle of poems called "The Road from Hiroshima") and Galway Kinnell and Carolyn Forché attempted to write as poets of the Nuclear Age, seeking a metaphor for the end of the world, and the lyric poems in Canto VII are my own efforts to speak (independently of those just mentioned) of nuclear disaster.

Forché's poem, "The Garden Shukkei-en," ends with a line of hope: "it is the bell to awaken God that we've heard ringing," and that bell rings for everyone.

Parallel to the American writing about Hiroshima has been the much greater quantity and intensity of the Japanese literature; and writer John Whittier Trent has surveyed Japanese Literature and the Atomic Bomb in *Writing Ground Zero* (1995). Attention must be given to Kenzaburo Oe's *Hiroshima Notes* (English translation 1963). For one like myself with no competence in the Japanese language (other that the dim memory of a wartime course in "Military Japanese") and limited reading of twentieth-century Japanese poetry, with even less of Japanese post-war fiction, it has been illuminating to have Masuji Ibuse's powerful novel about Hiroshima, *Black Rain*, placed meaningfully in its historical context by Trent.

I wish to add personal thanks to two friends who have contributed to my writing on Hiroshima. First, to Professor Paul A. Sawada, a colleague in Reformation scholarship, who corrected some of my historical details, especially about Nagasaki; and to Professor Elizabeth Schulz, a colleague at the University of Kansas, who gave me the benefit of her years of teaching in and visiting Japan, and her insight into the paper boats after the Hiroshima bombing has been incorporated gratefully into the texture of the poem. On a more personal note, Robert Calhoon, a fellow veteran of the 106th Signal Company, gave a reading of the penultimate draft of the poem that ultimate gift of total attention: he died, alas, before the poem had achieved its final form.

Finally, I am grateful to Associate Dean James Carothers and the Word Processing Center of the College of Liberal Arts and Sciences, University of Kansas, for their assistance in giving final shape to the manuscript.

R. J. S.

1945-1997
Lawrence, Kansas

---

* I have not used — I have not yet seen — a tool for research and teaching that should be recorded for possible use by students: "Critical Mass: America's Race to Build the Atom Bomb," for CD-ROM players used with Apple MacIntosh and IBM PC and compatibles. For it includes the story of events behind the Manhattan Project and biographies of the key scientists, together with film of the bombing of Nagasaki, as well as additional material. Produced by Corbis Corporation, 15395 SE 30th Place Suite 300, Bellevue, Wash. 98007.

ABOUT THE AUTHOR

Richard J. Schoeck was born in 1920 and graduated from Rumson High School, New Jersey, in 1936. After a few months at McGill University and several years in business, he enlisted in the Regular Army and served from 1940 to 1946.

He studied at Princeton University, where he earned an M.A. and Ph.D. in 1949. Thereafter he taught at Cornell, Notre Dame, Toronto, Washington and Colorado, with a final tenure of teaching American literature at the University of Trier. He has been a visiting lecturer or scholar at Yale, Princeton, Dallas, College of St. Thomas, and many other universities, as well as Bellagio, and Corpus Christi College, Oxford. For his scholarship he has received the Ford, Fulbright, Guggenheim and Canada Council fellowships, and he has been elected a Fellow of the Royal Society of Canada and the Royal Historical Society. Presently he is an Adjunct Professor of English at the University of Kansas, and he lives in Lawrence, Kansas, with his wife, Megan.

His publications include several hundred articles, papers and addresses, and a number of edited volumes. His own volumes include books on Sir Thomas More and Erasmus — with a two-volume biography of Erasmus published at Edinburgh in 1990-1993 — as well as two collections of poetry: *A Raging against Chaos* (London, 1989), and *The Eye of a Traveller* (Mellen Poetry Press, 1992).

ISBN 0-7734-2846-1